GREEN BERETS

SPECIAL FORCES: PROTECTING, BUILDING, TEACHING, AND FIGHTING

GREEN BERETS

by C. F. Earl

Mason Crest Publishers

MASON CREST PUBLISHERS INC.
370 Reed Road
Broomall, Pennsylvania 19008
(866)MCP-BOOK (toll free)
www.masoncrest.com

First Printing
9 8 7 6 5 4 3 2 1

Library of Congress Cataloging-in-Publication Data to come
Earl, C. F.
 Green Berets / by C.F. Earl.
      p. cm.
 Includes bibliographical references and index.
 ISBN 978-1-4222-1841-9
 ISBN (series) 978-1-4222-1836-5
 1. United States. Army. Special Forces–Juvenile literature. I. Title.
 UA34.S64E16 2011
 356'.167–dc22
                                    2010025293

Produced by Harding House Publishing Service, Inc.
www.hardinghousepages.com
Interior design by MK Bassett-Harvey.
Cover design by Torque Advertising + Design.
Printed in USA by Bang Printing.

With thanks and appreciation to the U.S. Military for the use of information, text, and images.

Contents

Introduction

lite forces are the tip of Freedom's spear. These small, special units are universally the first to engage, whether on reconnaissance missions into denied territory for larger conventional forces or in direct action, surgical operations, preemptive strikes, retaliatory action, and hostage rescues. They lead the way in today's war on terrorism, the war on drugs, the war on transnational unrest, and in humanitarian operations as well as nation building. When large-scale warfare erupts, they offer theater commanders a wide variety of unique, unconventional options.

Most such units are regionally oriented, acclimated to the culture and conversant in the languages of the areas where they operate. Since they deploy to those areas regularly, often for combined training exercises with indigenous forces, these elite units also serve as peacetime "global scouts," and "diplomacy multipliers," beacons of hope for the democratic aspirations of oppressed peoples all over the globe.

Elite forces are truly "quiet professionals": their actions speak louder than words. They are self-motivated, self-confidant, versatile, seasoned, mature individuals who rely on teamwork more than daring-do. Unfortunately, theirs is dangerous work. Since the 1980 attempt to rescue hostages from the U.S. embassy in Tehran, American special operations forces have suffered casualties in real-world operations at close to fifteen times the rate of U.S. conventional forces. By the very nature of the challenges that face special operations forces, training for these elite units has proven even more hazardous.

Thus it's with special pride that I join you in saluting the brave men who volunteer to serve in and support these magnificent units and who face such difficult challenges ahead.

—*Colonel John T. Carney, Jr., USAF–Ret.*
President, Special Operations Warrior Foundation

CHAPTER 1
The History of the United States Army

riginally formed in 1775, the United States Army has served in wars all over the world. Because its missions can take place anywhere in the world, U.S. Army soldiers must become experts in combat in a variety of scenarios, environments, and weather conditions.

The U.S. Army began as a force called the Continental Army in the late 1700s. At that time, the United States was facing the turmoil of revolution. The British rulers had placed harsh laws upon the American colonies, and a group of American leaders gathered to work out how they would achieve independence.

At a meeting called the Second Continental Congress, held on June 14, 1775, the Continental Army was formed under the command of George Washington, who would go on to be America's first Commander in Chief. During the

Revolutionary War, between 1775 and 1783, the Continental Army fought against the British. Originally only 960 men strong, the Continental Army was to be the seed from which the modern U.S. Army would grow.

After the Revolutionary War was won, the Continental Army was disbanded. With independence achieved, the United States Army now took over. The President of the United States was the power behind the Army, the Commander in Chief of all armed forces serving the new nation. As Commander in Chief, the President could order the Army into battle whenever he felt military force was necessary. Ultimately, the country could not afford to keep a large standing military at all times during the early days of both the Army and the nation. At that time, the U.S. Army grew or shrank in size depending on whether or not the country was at war.

Over the next century, the United States Army would be tested in wide range of combat situations. During the War of 1812, the Army was once again fighting the British, in addition to Native American tribes funded and equipped by the British Empire. From 1846 to 1848, U.S. Army soldiers fought in Mexico. The biggest leap for the U.S. Army happened between 1861 and 1865 during the American Civil War. Remarkably, the U.S. Army expanded during the four years of civil war to become a massive fighting force of around one million men.

After another fifty years of changes in size and organization, in 1917, the U.S. Army entered World War I. Europe had been locked in blood battle for nearly three years, and Britain, France, and their allies were almost exhausted. With

The courage and efforts of the Continental Army was what earned the United States its freedom.

over three and a half million men in its ranks, and some of the most advanced military equipment available, the United States arrived in battle as one of the best trained and pre-pared armies in the world at the time. During World War I, the Army fought hard, losing thousands of men before 1918, when the war ended in German defeat and victory for America and her European allies.

World War II had been raging across Europe since 1939, but in 1941 when the Japanese bombed the U.S. fleet sta-

The attack on Pearl Harbor triggered America's involvement in World War II.

tioned at Pearl Harbor in Hawaii, the United States entered the war. Millions of men across the United States were called up to serve in the Army, and it grew to over eight million men. These men served across the globe—in Japan and the Pacific, Africa, and Europe. They fought huge battles with German and Japanese forces. Tough and experienced German units were amazed at how quickly U.S. recruits became hard fighting soldiers, and the U.S. contribution to the war meant that victory for the Allies was certain. Both Germany and Japan surrendered in 1945, after the Allies stormed Berlin and the United States dropped two atomic bombs on the Japanese cities of Hiroshima and Nagasaki. During World War II, the U.S. Army was also reorganized into different parts—each part called a Command. There were Army Ground Forces, Army Air Forces (the Air Force would become separate in 1947), and Army Service Forces. The Women's Army Corps was also formed in 1942.

World War II proved what a remarkable fighting force the U.S. Army had become since its birth before the Revolutionary War, but many wars have also tested the Army from that time until now. Between 1950 and 1953, the Army was engaged in the Korean War, fighting Communist North Korean forces invading the South. Starting in 1955, U.S. Army soldiers also fought Communist forces in the Vietnam War, combating the **guerrilla** tactics of the Viet Cong. Through the end of the war in 1975, when the capital of South Vietnam, Saigon,

UNDERSTAND THE FULL MEANING

guerrilla: A style of warfare that makes use of sabotage, harassment, and surprise attacks.

was taken by the Communist North Vietnamese Army, the U.S. Army served valiantly, attempting to halt the spread of Communism. American Army soldiers also fought in Operation Desert Storm, driving invading Iraqi Army forces from Kuwait. Throughout the 1990s, the U.S. Army was involved in a variety of peacekeeping missions around the world. Since the terrorist attacks of September 11, 2001, the Army has been involved in both the wars in Afghanistan and Iraq.

Today, the Army is one of the three military departments that report to the United States' Department of Defense, along with the Navy and Air Force. More than one million Americans are serving in the modern Army, Army National Guard, and Army Reserves. In 2009, the Army requested more than $140 billion for its budget, making it one of the largest military organizations in history.

The Army's mission is "to fight and win the Nation's wars by providing prompt, sustained land dominance across the

UNDERSTAND THE FULL MEANING

spectrum: A range or sequence.

policy: A high-level overall plan that includes the general goals and acceptable procedures, especially of a governmental body.

strategic: Having to do with what's necessary to carry out a plan of action.

infrastructure: The underlying framework or structure.

deploy: To place military units in battle formation or in appropriate position.

humanitarian: Promoting human well-being.

full range of military operations and **spectrum** of conflict in support of combatant commanders." The Army is responsible for protecting the United States of America and its global interests, be they **policy** oriented or **strategic** in nature. The Army is capable of waging war and keeping the peace, all the while remaining ready for any military scenario.

The Army is made up of two distinct and equally important parts: the active components and the reserve components, the United States Army Reserve and the Army National Guard. Regardless of which component, there are two types of missions that the Army conducts: operational and institu tional. The operational army consists of numbered armies, corps, divisions, brigades, and battalions that conduct full-spectrum operations all around the world. The institutional Army supports the operational Army by providing the **infra-structure** necessary to raise, train, equip, **deploy**, and ensure the readiness of all Army forces; it also allows the Army to expand rapidly in time of war. Without the institutional Army, the operational Army cannot function; without the operational Army, the institutional Army has no purpose.

In the twenty-first century, the men and women of the United States Army work tirelessly to combat threats to American national security. Serving in the wars in Iraq and Afghanistan, as well as in a **humanitarian** capacity around the world (most recently after the earthquakes in Haiti in January 2010), the U.S. Army is one of the strongest , best trained, and most effective military units that the world has ever known.

CHAPTER 2

History of the U.S. Army Special Forces

The Army Special Forces (often nicknamed the Green Berets) were formed to give the U.S. Army an **elite** unit that could operate behind enemy lines. Their role was to fight a special sort of war known as "counter-insurgency." This included **sabotage**, **reconnaissance**, guerrilla warfare, and teaching other armies and civilians how to fight.

During the Korean War (1950–53), elite soldiers were used, but often they were not official units. However, on June 18, 1952, the Tenth Special Forces Group (Airborne)—

UNDERSTAND THE FULL MEANING

elite: A group or class of people who are superior in quality to others.

sabotage: To destroy an enemy's property or hinder the enemy's normal operations.

reconnaissance: Scouting and exploring to gain information about an enemy.

known as the SFGA—was created. Its job was intended to be "special missions" in the case of war in Europe between the **communist** Soviet Union and the West. It was based at Fort Bragg, North Carolina, a training base that eventually became the John F. Kennedy Special Warfare School. During the 1950s and early 1960s, the communists expanded in many other areas around the world. Many governments were overthrown by communist revolutions. To U.S. military officers, the map of the world in the Pentagon appeared to be slowly turning communist-red.

Because of this, teaching at the Special Warfare School became more specialized, concentrating on how to fight communist guerrillas but also turn the civilian populations against them and win their support. President John F. Kennedy was particularly enthusiastic about the Special Forces. War had begun in Vietnam against undercover communist fighters, and Kennedy felt that these tough new American soldiers could be the key to victory. Kennedy himself formally gave them their first green berets, and since then, Special Forces soldiers have been known around the world for their green berets. While many Special Forces teams were sent to Vietnam at that time, other Green Berets were sent to Africa, the Middle East, and Latin America

One of the Special Forces' most important missions in the Vietnam War was training South Vietnamese military forces and civilians to fight the Vietnamese communists, known as the Viet Cong. But they were not only there to help people

UNDERSTAND THE FULL MEANING

communist: A totalitarian system of government.

A Viet Cong soldier, one of the communist-backed troops in Vietnam.

fight. They also helped the South Vietnamese people to live better lives and have better facilities. This was intended to make sure the Vietnamese supported the United States more than they supported the Viet Cong. The Special Forces achieved incredible things, creating:

- 129 churches
- 110 hospitals
- 1,003 classrooms
- 398 medical clinics
- 272 markets
- 6,436 wells
- 1,500 miles of road
- 14,934 transportation depots

In addition, the Green Berets provided support to about half a million Vietnamese refugees.

However, the Green Berets were also tough warriors, and they took the fight to the Viet Cong with incredible skill and ruthlessness. Teamed up with the Vietnamese people they had trained, the Green Berets went deep into the jungle-covered mountains of Vietnam to destroy enemy bases with lightning speed before disappearing back into the under-growth as if they had never existed. The communists fought back. On one occasion, one thousand Viet Cong guerrillas came together to assault the Special Forces camp at Nam Dong, a remote base far from any support. The attack began

Fighting was not the only thing the U.S. military did during the Vietnam War; American soldiers also partnered with the Vietnamese people on building projects and rescue missions.

President John F. Kennedy and the Green Berets

Special Forces soldiers first wore the green beret in 1953, though, at that time, the Army refused to allow it to be worn in any official capacity. Initially, the berets were worn by a few detachments, but soon many in the Special Forces were wearing it during long exercises in the field.

In 1961, President John F. Kennedy scheduled a visit to Fort Bragg, where many Special Forces units were stationed. Before his arrival, he told Brigadier General William P. Yarborough (Special Forces Warfare Center commander at the time) that all Special Forces soldiers should wear their berets for the event. The President felt that, due to the special nature of Special Forces missions, Special Forces soldiers should have some way of distinguishing themselves from their fellow soldiers. The Department of Army had already, however, sent a message to the Center making the green berets an official part of the Special Forces uniform, ahead of Kennedy's visit.

Wearing his green beret, General Yarborough welcomed President Kennedy to Fort Bragg on October 12,

at 2:30 a.m. on July 6, 1964. Within hours, the camp was ablaze as white phosphorous shells—a ferocious explosive that sends out showers of white flame—rained down on the base. Two hours later, a helicopter gunship arrived ahead of reinforcements. Inside the camp, fifty-five soldiers lay dead, with another sixty-five wounded, but Captain Roger Donlon,

1961. The President said, "Those are nice. How do you like the green beret?"

"They're fine, sir. We've wanted them a long time," Yarborough replied.

Later that day, President Kennedy wrote a personal message to General Yarborough. It said, in part, "My congratulations to you personally for your part in the presentation today. . . . The challenge of this old but new form of operations is a real one and I know that you and the members of your command will carry on for us and the free world in a manner which is both worthy and inspiring. I am sure that the green beret will be a mark of distinction in the trying times ahead."

A few months later, on April 11, 1962, in a White House memorandum sent to the Army, President Kennedy called the green beret "a symbol of excellence, a badge of courage, a mark of distinction in the fight for freedom."

To this day, the Special Forces have a deep connection to President Kennedy for his commitment to their mission. Each year on the date of his assassination (November 22nd), Special Forces soldiers pay tribute to President Kennedy by laying a wreath and green beret on his tomb.

a Special Forces commander, continued to lead the fight, despite being wounded in the stomach. His bravery and outstanding leadership won him the Congressional Medal of Honor.

The Special Forces not only knew how to take the war to the Viet Cong, but they also succeeded in turning the tactics of guerrilla warfare against the enemy. Patrols were sent out to act like bait to the VC. When the communists ambushed the patrols, they themselves fell into a trap set by the Special Forces. Another special job for the Green Berets was rescuing U.S. soldiers from the hands of the communists, particularly airmen who had been shot down. This program was called "Bright Light." There were two types of Bright Light missions. The first was designed to recover personnel who found themselves evading capture behind enemy lines (called "evaders"). The second type was aimed at rescuing American Prisoners of War (POWs) being held by the Viet Cong.

Overall, the Vietnam War showed the world what elite warriors the Green Berets really were. But Vietnam was not the only place where they were in action. In 1961, Green Berets had begun conducting military operations in Latin America. As in Vietnam, the Special Forces in Latin America were mainly there to train local soldiers to fight more effectively. From 1955 to 1969, U.S. aid helped establish Peruvian **commando** battalions, Chilean Special Forces and Airborne Units, as well as Special Forces (Airborne) groups and elite infantry in the Dominican Republic, Venezuela, Bolivia, and Columbia. Many of these countries also raised police commando units for urban counterterrorist operations. Another unit to emerge from the Special Forces was one specialized in counterterrorism and hostage-rescue. This secret

UNDERSTAND THE FULL MEANING

commando: A military unit trained and organized as shock troops, especially for hit-and-run raids into enemy territory.

Green Berets in Vietnam.

Bronze Bruce: The Special Warfare Memorial Statue

Known as Bronze Bruce, the Special Warfare Memorial Statue was the first memorial to soldiers who served in the Vietnam War in the United States. Since its dedication in 1969, the statue has become the focal point of the Army Special Operations Command's Memorial Plaza at Fort Bragg in North Carolina. A Green Beret was chosen to serve as the model for the statue in light of the fact that almost all the Army Special Operations soldiers who lost their lives in Vietnam were Special Forces soldiers. Though the statue depicts a Green Beret, it is symbolic of all soldiers who conduct, or have conducted, special operations for the U.S. Army.

The statue itself is twelve feet tall, though the pedestal on which it stands brings the height of the memorial to twenty-two feet total. Dressed in the jungle uniform Special Forces soldiers wore during the Vietnam War, the statue is a testament to what it means to be a member of the U.S. Army Special Forces. The soldier depicted in the statue wears the rank of sergeant first class and holds an M-16 rifle in his right hand. The M-16 was a standard weapon used by the Green Berets in Vietnam. Importantly, his finger is not on the trigger but at the ready. The

unit was designed to be similar to the elite British force, the Special Air Service (SAS). It specialized in daring undercover operations against terrorists, and also fast action to release hostages held at gunpoint.

soldier is ready for oncoming threats, but primarily, as is the case with all Green Berets, he is serving to keep the peace and make connections with those in need around the world. To the soldiers serving in the Special Forces, the Special Warfare Memorial Statue is the embodiment of the Green Berets' mission of liberating the oppressed peoples of the world, a symbol that inspires today's Special Forces soldiers to do the same.

Within the base of the statue, a time capsule contains a Special Forces uniform, green beret, a bust of President John F. Kennedy, and a copy of his speech commemorating the official acceptance of the green beret.

The cost of the memorial statue was approximately $100,000 in 1969. To provide the money for the statue, Special Forces soldiers from across the globe donated around $89,000; large donations from public figures key to the history of the Green Berets provided the rest. John Wayne, the famous film actor, donated five thousand dollars after he starred and co directed the 1968 move *The Green Berets*. Barry Sadler, who composed a song called "Ballad of the Green Berets," also donated five thousand dollars toward the creation of the Special Warfare Memorial Statue. The secretary of defense at the time, Robert McNamara, donated one thousand dollars.

Throughout the 1970s and 1980s, the Special Forces found themselves conducting many secret operations in Latin America against communist governments or guerrillas. The Green Berets were also involved in the 1983 invasion

The AC-130 gunship is a heavily-armed ground-attack airplane.
Green Berets and other Special Forces used it for the invasion of Iraq.

of Grenada and the 1991 Gulf War. In Grenada, a secret unit was given the job of assaulting Richmond Hill Prison on the western side of the island and rescuing the prisoners, who would then be evacuated by helicopter. Unfortunately, the helicopter assault was delayed, and by the time the unit reached the prison, the opposition had fully alerted their antiaircraft batteries. One UH0-60 Black Hawk helicopter was shot down and the rest driven off by the hail of fire, bringing the unit's involvement in Operation Urgent Fury to a difficult end.

After Iraq invaded Kuwait on August 2, 1990, U.S. Special Forces were among the first units to be deployed to Saudi Arabia as part of Operation Desert Shield. Immediately, they began training for operations deep inside Iraqi territory. They also trained personnel from the Saudi armed forces and the Kuwaiti resistance. The latter were taught how to ambush Iraqi units inside Kuwait, and to collect and pass on important **intelligence**.

Before the Allied land assault began on February 24, 1991, American Special Forces had gone into enemy territory in Iraq and Kuwait and were conducting a wide variety of missions. These included destroying Iraqi radars to protect the Allied fighters and bombers, which were attacking the Iraqi army. In addition, Special Forces teams also saved Allied aircrew who had been shot down, and then guarded them until they could be evacuated by helicopter. Other roles included sabotage, ambushes, and intelligence

UNDERSTAND THE FULL MEANING

intelligence: Information concerning an enemy.

This is one of the many refugee camps in Haiti where people devastated by the January 2010 earthquake took shelter. The Green Berets were there to help them.

gathering. The Special Forces' fast-attack vehicle (FAV) was first used operationally in the Gulf War. This is a rugged buggy that can be driven at high speeds across the tough desert landscape. It is armed with machine guns, grenade launchers, and other weapons, and the Special Forces used it to devastating effect against Iraqi positions.

Today, the Green Berets are on standby, ready to respond to any emergency, such as the terrorist attacks on New York and Washington, D.C., in September 2001. The John F. Kennedy Special Warfare Center and School (SWCS) continues to oversee all aspects of Green Beret training. In the modern wars in Iraq and Afghanistan, the Green Berets have been called to execute vital and dangerous missions key to securing American objectives. The Special Forces are also working around the world to train foreign military units in the kinds of tactics in which they specialize and deliver humanitarian support to a variety of aid efforts around the globe, including relief efforts in Haiti after the January 2010 earthquake.

CHAPTER 3
Today's U.S. Army Special Forces

The U.S. Army Special Forces Command (SFC), itself overseen by the U.S. Army Special Operations Command (USASOC), oversees today's Special Forces. Special Forces Command is in charge of five active Special Forces Groups (SFG), in addition to two Army National Guard groups. Each Special Forces Group is positioned so it can support one of the U.S. military commands located around the world. These commands each have their own missions, responsibilities, and leadership, and work with the Special Forces in different capacities, depending on their needs. The United States' commands include:

- U.S. European Command
- U.S. Atlantic Command
- U.S. Pacific Command

- U.S. Southern Command
- U.S. Central Command

In the November 1990, the U.S. Army First Special Operations Command was renamed the U.S. Army Special Forces Command (Airborne) (USASFC(A)). Special Forces Command is responsible for the training and preparation of Special Forces soldiers. SFC must ensure that the Army's Special Forces are able to carry out missions successfully, no matter when or where they are deployed. Unlike any other unit of similar size, USASFC(A) is spread across the country—on both coasts of the United States—as well as around the world.

OPERATIONAL DETACHMENTS

A Special Forces Group is made up of a headquarters company, a group support company, and three Special Forces battalions. Every Special Forces company is assigned six Operational Detachment Alphas (ODAs). The ODA is the main unit of Special Forces operations in the U.S. Army.

OPERATIONAL DETACHMENT A (ODA)

Called Operational Detachment Alpha (ODA) (or A-Teams), these twelve-man **detachments** are the smallest within the Special Forces structure. A-Teams consist of two leader-

UNDERSTAND THE FULL MEANING

detachments: Military units.

A Special Forces group do reconnaissance in the remote Shok Valley of Afghanistan where they fought an almost seven-hour battle with terrorists in a mountainside village.

ship positions (Commanding Officer and Warrant Officer, the second in command), and ten soldiers filling five specialist positions (two soldiers per specialization). The specialist positions within an A-Team include Intelligence and

U.S. Army Special Forces Groups:

Active Groups:

1st Special Forces Group (Airborne): Fort Lewis, Washington

One battalion in Okinawa, Japan

3rd Special Forces Group (Airborne): Fort Bragg, North Carolina

5th Special Forces Group (Airborne): Fort Campbell, Kentucky

7th Special Forces Group (Airborne): Eglin Air Force Base, Florida

10th Special Forces Group (Airborne): Fort Carson, Colorado

One battalion in Stuttgart, Germany

National Guard Groups:

19th Special Forces Group (Airborne): Draper, Utah

20th Special Forces Group (Airborne): Birmingham, Alabama

Operations Sergeant, Communications Sergeant, Medical Officer, Weapons Sergeant and Engineer Sergeant. Two Green Berets serve in each nonleadership position within an A-Team so that the group may split into two if need be.

The positions within an A-Team are as follows:

- The Commanding Officer and the Warrant Officer make leadership decisions throughout the mission, and must be prepared to adapt and change plans as necessary. A-Teams regularly fight alongside local forces when serving overseas, and in these cases the Commanding and Warrant Officers may be responsible for leading these makeshift units. In addition, they may advise local leaders or officials.

- Intelligence and Operations Sergeants collect and interpret intelligence on territories the A-Team occupies and on the enemy. These solders are also responsible for outfitting the detachment with the supplies and equipment they need for the mission at hand.

- Communications Sergeants are in charge of the communications equipment that the ODA carries. These soldiers are also responsible for relaying any information gathered by the Intelligence Sergeants back to Special Operations Command (SOCOM).

- Medical Officers are prepared to perform surgery in the field, set up **improvised** hospitals, offer medical treatment to local populations, and give medical care to the detachment. Medical Officers receive ten months of medical training in addition to the regular training that all Green Berets go through.

UNDERSTAND THE FULL MEANING

improvised: Made use of whatever is available.

- Weapons Sergeants are trained to use the weapons of the U.S. military. In addition, these soldiers are also able to train others, including armies assembled by the team or foreign military forces, in how to utilize certain weapons.

- Engineer Sergeants serve as navigators for the A-Team. They also design any structures needed in the field, including improvised bridges if the need arises. These soldiers are trained in demolitions and sabotage, as well.

Each Special Forces company is made up of six A-Teams. Of these six, one team is trained to specialize in airborne insertion by parachute, while another team is trained in underwater insertion. All A-Teams are experts in **infiltration** by land and are able to get behind enemy lines without being detected.

OPERATIONAL DETACHMENT B (ODB)

The Special Forces company headquarters is known as "B Detachment." Though it cannot deploy its own Special Forces teams without assistance, it supports teams in the field and on base.

OPERATIONAL DETACHMENT C (ODC)

Called "C Detachment," ODC commands, supervises, and administrates the organization of a specific Special Forces

UNDERSTAND THE FULL MEANING

infiltration: The process of getting into enemy territory.

battalion. C Detachment plans Special Forces operations, assists soldiers in planning their military careers, and supports Special Forces soldiers by carrying out all planning duties for the battalion. ODC is also responsible for directing the successful execution of these plans.

The Special Forces do far more than just fight. This member of the Army Special Forces is giving a vitamin shot to a rooster in the Philippines, as part of the veterinarian services his troop provided to farmers living near the Army base.

SPECIAL FORCES MISSIONS

The U.S. Army Special Forces are trained and equipped for several specific kinds of missions. These include:

- **unconventional** warfare
- foreign internal defense
- special reconnaissance
- direct action
- combating terrorism
- **counter-proliferation**
- information operations

The U.S. Army Special Forces are unique in the U.S. military in that they are required to carry out missions in times of war and peace.

Unconventional warfare is one of the main missions for which the Green Berets are responsible. Regular tactics cannot be used during unconventional warfare missions, making the Green Berets all the more prized by the U.S. military for their skill and experience with these **tactics**.

UNDERSTAND THE FULL MEANING

unconventional: Not following the usual ways of doing things; in warfare, using indirect methods of fighting.

counter-proliferation: Referring to working to slow or stop the production and distribution of weapons, both conventional weapons and weapons of mass destruction.

tactics: Specific maneuvers to achieve goals.

Unlike quick direct action operations, unconventional warfare (including tactics like guerrilla warfare) can last for long periods of time, during which the Green Berets will recruit local forces to their side, training civilians to take up arms if need be. These tactics are employed behind enemy lines, making these missions dangerous but vital to setting up later military operations. For instance, Green Berets may build relationships with local leaders and military forces

Special Forces are trained to do their work in any environment. Here, Green Berets are conducting the culmination exercise of a five-day cold-weather exposure training course.

Special Forces Creed:

- I am an American Special Forces Soldier!

- I will do all that my nation requires of me. I am a volunteer, knowing well the hazards of my profession.

- I serve with the memory of those who have gone before me. I pledge to uphold the honor and integrity of their legacy in all that I am—in all that I do.

- I am a warrior. I will teach and fight whenever and wherever my nation requires. I will strive always to excel in every art and artifice of war.

- I know that I will be called upon to perform tasks in isolation, far from familiar faces and voices. With the help and guidance of my faith, I will conquer my fears and succeed.

- I will keep my mind and body clean, alert, and strong. I will maintain my arms and equipment in an immaculate state befitting a Special Forces Soldier, for this is my debt to those who depend upon me.

- I will not fail those with whom I serve. I will not bring shame upon myself or Special Forces.

- I will never leave a fallen comrade. I will never surrender though I am the last. If I am taken, I pray that I have the strength to defy my enemy.

- I am a member of my Nation's chosen soldiery, I serve quietly, not seeking recognition or accolades. My goal is to succeed in my mission—and live to succeed again.

in enemy territory in order to later use these relationships against the enemy.

A tactic called Foreign Internal Defense is the main mission of the U.S. Army Special Forces during times of peace. These operations are designed to help American **allies** develop their military and police forces. This includes training them in tactics and technical skills. In addition, Foreign Internal Defense covers many kinds of humanitarian aid missions, in which Special Forces soldiers assist in disaster relief or community development. Special Forces units may also be called upon to carry out search-and-rescue missions and a variety of counter-drug operations, as well as other peacetime actions

Special Forces soldiers support **coalition** forces fighting the wars in Iraq and Afghanistan. First emerging as a central Special Forces mission during the Gulf War, coalition support became a primary mission of the Green Berets due to the large number of foreign troops working together in both exercises and operations. Green Berets, who all must know a foreign language and be able to communicate across cultural barriers, are ideal candidates for the kind of work that fighting with a coalition of nations requires of America's soldiers.

UNDERSTAND THE FULL MEANING

allies: People, groups, or nations that work together for a common purpose.

coalition: An alliance or an organization of countries united by a pact or treaty.

CHAPTER 4
Training

.S. Army Special Forces soldiers are among the most highly skilled, well-educated soldiers in the world. Not only must these soldiers be proficient in combat, they must also know a second language, be able to communicate across cultural lines, and act as America's ambassadors on the world stage. Soldiers must complete combat, parachute, survival, and language training courses in order to earn their place in the Special Forces.

All Green Berets begin their careers in the Army with the same basic training all enlisted soldiers must complete. From that point forward, however, Special Forces candidates are offered many special opportunities to receive training that other soldiers are not. This includes training at the U.S. Army Airborne School, and training at the prestigious John F. Kennedy Special Warfare Center and School.

Special Forces training is designed to test the mental and physical endurance of each soldier, to measure whether or not he has what it takes to become a Green Beret. Candidates for the Special Forces will need to exhibit teamwork, maturity, intelligence, fitness, and motivation in order to be successful in this training. Only the best of the best will become Green Berets and serve as part of the U.S. Army Special Forces.

Over the course of their training, Green Beret candidates must complete the following:

Special Operations Preparation Course (SOPC)

Special Forces Assessment and Selection (SFAS)

Special Forces Qualification Course (SFQC)

Live Environment Training (LET)

U.S. ARMY AIRBORNE SCHOOL

All Green Berets must qualify for and complete training at the U.S. Army Airborne School, located at Fort Benning, Georgia, before they can move to Special Forces training. During their Airborne training, soldiers make their way through three stages of intense training, preparing for the final stage, in which they make five training jumps from a plane more than a thousand feet in the air.

The First Battalion (Airborne), 507th Infantry Regiment has the task of operating and maintaining the U.S Army Airborne School, where soldiers who have completed Basic Combat Training learn to operate parachutes and complete parachute jumps in preparation for the missions they will carry out as Army Rangers. The Airborne School instructors

Bradley Chanady jumps from a 34-foot tower at Mann Field, Fort Benning, Georgia. Three hundred soldiers from the 173 Airborne Brigade Combat Team traveled from Bamberg and Schweinfurt, Germany, and Vicenza, Italy, to go through Airborne School at Fort Benning.

A student practices proper landing techniques on the Swing Landing Trainer.

wear black berets and are known around the world as "black hats." These instructors come from the Army, Marine Corps, Navy, and Air Force.

The First Battalion is divided into six companies. The first, Headquarters Company, is responsible for organizing the

Airborne School and carrying out administration duties for the First Battalion. Four companies (A, B, C, and D Companies) provide instruction for the soldiers going through the Basic Airborne Course. Finally, E Company assists the battalion and soldiers utilize parachute equipment, and also provides assistance when needed.

Students at the Airborne School receive instruction from the same sergeants and leaders throughout the three phases of training. This strategy of teaching is employed in order to maximize unit cohesion and mitigate discipline problems.

Training at the Airborne School lasts three weeks, one for each phase of training.

GROUND WEEK

During Ground Week, students learn the skills they'll need in order to make their first parachute jump. Students complete exercises using a variety of towers and what is called a mock door, a version of a plane door used for training. To move forward in their Airborne training, soldiers must complete jumps from test towers and pass all physical requirements for the Airborne School.

AIRBORNE TOWER WEEK

After completing Ground Week, students at Airborne School continue their training during Airborne Tower Week. In addition to honing their jump skills using towers and mock jumps, Tower Week also introduces the notion of "mass exit"— many soldiers orderly jumping from a single plane door as efficiently as possible. In order to master this operation, students use the mock door at the top of a tower for mass exit training exercises. During Tower Week, students must jump from 34- and 250-foot towers.

AIRBORNE JUMP WEEK

Once Airborne School students have finished both Ground and Tower Week, they are prepared to move onto Jump Week, the final phase of their Airborne training. During Jump Week, students must complete five parachute jumps from aircraft flying at 1,250 feet. Two of these jumps are called combat equipment jumps, in which students must complete a jump successfully in full combat gear (and while carrying a fake weapon). The other three jumps are known as "Hollywood" jumps, and only require that students jump with a parachute and reserve chute. One of the five mandatory jumps is usually conducted at night, though a night jump is not mandatory if Jump Week includes a three day federal holiday weekend and a night jump is not possible due to scheduling.

GRADUATION

The Airborne School's graduation ceremony is usually held at nine o'clock in the morning on the Friday of Jump Week. Occasionally, students may graduate immediately after finishing their final jump, right on the drop zone (DZ), should weather or other issue cause cancellation or potential delay of the normal ceremony. Family and friends of Airborne School students are permitted to come to the graduation ceremony, and even watch some of the jumps students complete from the DZ.

SPECIAL OPERATIONS PREPARATION COURSE (SOPC)

The SOPC is a thirty-day course conducted at Fort Bragg, designed to prepare soldiers for the Special Forces Assessment and Selection Course. Soldiers will receive physical training and instruction on land navigation, a vital skill for

Paratrooper students exit from the tailgate of an Air Force C-130 Hercules cargo plane during a training exercise.

all Green Berets. Successful completion of SOPC does not guarantee that soldiers will complete the next section of Special Forces training.

SPECIAL FORCES ASSESSMENT AND SELECTION (SFAS)

Held at Camp Mackall, near Fort Bragg in North Carolina, the Special Forces Assessment and Selection program consists of twenty-four days of intense survival and fitness training. Special Forces Candidates must exhibit intelligence, **resourcefulness**, and an ability to adapt. SFAS is made to measure how well a candidate would stand up to Special Forces training. From the time they arrive at the program until the time they leave, the candidates' superiors are evaluating them. They are judged for twelve attributes: intelligence, physical fitness, motivation, trustworthiness, **accountability**, maturity, **stability**, judgment, **decisiveness**, teamwork, influence, and communications. Land navigation is a major focus in Special Forces Assessment and Selection. The program also includes a one-mile obstacle course, a variety of runs, road marches, and rappelling exercises.

Those who complete SFAS will have the opportunity to continue their Special Forces training in the Qualifications Course. A board of officers review soldiers' performance during the Special Forces Assessment and Selection program, evaluating whether or not they are prepared for Special Forces training. Of the 1,800 candidates who go through SFAS, only around 40 percent of all candidates are successful.

SPECIAL FORCES QUALIFICATIONS COURSE (SFQC)

The Special Forces Qualifications Course is made up of five phases (phases II–VI of Special Forces training). Upon completion of the SFQC, soldiers will become members of the U.S. Army Special Forces. Soldiers who have graduated from SFQC are some of the Army's foremost experts in what the military calls unconventional warfare (tactics that involve quickly striking at the enemy, often with element of surprise). The five phases of the Special Forces Qualifications Course (SFQC) are:

INDIVIDUAL SKILL

During the second phase of Special Forces training, called the individual phase, Green Beret candidates will receive instruction and training in navigation on land and small unit tactics. This phase also includes training exercises involving

UNDERSTAND THE FULL MEANING

resourcefulness: The ability to cope with difficult situations by coming up with new ideas on your own.

accountability: The ability to be responsible to someone for your actions.

stability: The quality of being steadfast and firm, not easily shaken.

decisiveness: The ability to make decisions easily.

Even when they have completed their training, Green Berets are expected to continuously upgrade their skills. Here, Green Beret troops go on a practice search patrol through the woods.

these skills, as well as the use of live ammunition during some exercises.

MILITARY OCCUPATIONAL SPECIALTY (MOS) TRAINING

During the MOS training phase (phase III of Special Forces training), soldiers are instructed on one of a number of specialty skills. These educational specializations are based on soldiers' interests and talents, as well as their ambitions for the future. Military Occupational Specialties available to Special Forces trainees include everything from engineering to infantry training. While some MOS training programs are based on military specializations, many are applicable to civilian life as well.

COLLECTIVE TRAINING

Collective training (phase IV of Special Forces training) focuses on training soldiers in organization, unconventional warfare operations, direct-action operations, and some airborne operations. Special Forces trainees deploy to Uwharrie National Forest, North Carolina, for an exercise in Unconventional Warfare. In the forest, soldiers serve as a member of an Operational Detachment Alpha (ODA). During this exercise, specialty and common skills are evaluated.

LANGUAGE TRAINING

Language training is an essential part of the Special Forces Qualification Course. All Green Berets must be fluent in a foreign language. Soldiers have the opportunity to study Arabic, Spanish, Chinese, and Russian, as well as many other languages. Language training is phase V of Special Forces training.

SERE COURSE

The Survival, Evasion, Resistance, and Escape (SERE) course is the final stage in the SFQC portion of Special Forces training (phase VI). In addition to training in wilderness survival, the SERE course also prepares soldiers to resist enemy **interrogation** and escape capture should they be taken prisoner.

LIVE ENVIRONMENT TRAINING

All Special Forces soldiers must also receive training that involves immersion in a foreign culture. Soldiers will learn the language, customs, and traditions of the country in which they undergo Live Environment Training. This kind of preparation is a core part of what it is to be a Green Beret. Special Forces soldiers must be experts in both combat and working with people of other countries and cultures around the world.

JOHN F. KENNEDY SPECIAL WARFARE CENTER AND SCHOOL

MISSION

The John F. Kennedy Special Warfare Center and School is responsible for recruiting, training, and educating the U.S. Army Special Forces. The school also provides Special Forces

UNDERSTAND THE FULL MEANING

interrogation: The act of officially questioning someone.

Intensive language training, organized by the Defense Language Institute Foreign Language Center, begins with students spending four days a week, six hours a day with native Afghan instructors, learning how to read, write, learn tactical vocabulary, and construct sentences.

trainees with advanced skills courses. It is up to the Special Warfare Center and School (SWCS) to equip Special Forces soldiers with the skills they will require to carry out some of the most difficult special operations missions. Lastly, the SWCS assists soldiers in managing their military careers, advising them about their options.

The JFK Special Warfare Center and School aims to be the world's finest Special Operations Forces training center. SWCS works to stay current in all its training procedures, educational courses, and administrative policies so that its students always learn the most modern and relevant information. This allows the Green Berets to remain a flexible force, able to adapt to a changing wartime environment.

OVERVIEW

The John F. Kennedy Special Warfare Center and School is the Army's special operations training university. The SWCS is responsible for special operations training and developing Special Forces leadership. The center and school's training group conducts a wide variety of special operations training. In addition, SWCS assists in testing new equipment. Each year, the school trains more than 10,000 U.S. and foreign students in sixty-eight programs.

The only place in the world soldiers can earn the right to wear the green beret is at the John F. Kennedy Special Warfare Center and School at Fort Bragg, North Carolina.

HISTORY

In 1951, the SWCS began as the Psychological Warfare Division of the Army General School at Fort Riley, Kansas. A year

A Green Beret climbs Castle Rock near Leavenworth, Washington, part of a group that conducted military mountaineering training to maintain the skills that allow them to reach their objectives in mountainous terrain anywhere in the world.

later, in 1952, the school moved to Fort Bragg. Almost a decade after that, in 1961, the school established the Special Forces Training Group in order to train enlisted soldiers for assignments in Special Forces' groups. On October 1, 1983, the Institute for Military Assistance at Fort Bragg, North Carolina was renamed the JFK Special Warfare Center, as a result of a special operations forces' reorganization that year. Originally, the Special Warfare Center was set up as a branch of the U.S. Army Training and Doctrine Command (TRADOC), classified as a special training activity. In June of 1990, however, during changes to the organization of Special Operations Forces, the school became part of Special Operations Command. The Joint Special Operations Medical Training Center at the school, created in 1996, is responsible for standardizing all Special Operations Forces medical training.

FIRST SPECIAL WARFARE TRAINING GROUP

The First Special Warfare Training Group is at the center of all Special Forces training. This group conducts the Special Forces Assessment and Selection Course, Special Forces Qualification Course, and all advanced Special Forces skills training, including language training and regional studies.

The First Special Warfare Training Group (Airborne) is responsible for all six phases of Special Forces training during the Qualification Course. In order to meet this challenge, the group divides the responsibility into several battalions. First Battalion is responsible for all field training that takes place during Special Forces training. Third Battalion instructs students during language training, while Fourth Battalion is responsible for all military occupational specialty (MOS) training. Company B, Second Battalion, operates the Military Free Fall School, which prepares Special Forces trainees to execute parachute jumps. Company C, Second Battalion, operates the Special Forces Underwater Operations School in Key West, Florida.

Training to become a Green Beret is not easy. It's a long, challenging road—but those who have the stamina, intelligence, and courage to reach the end of that road are well prepared to carry out some of the most important military missions in the world.

CHAPTER 5
Modern Missions

Today's Special Forces are actively engaged in a variety of missions in support of U.S. foreign policy or strategic objectives. Whether training and assisting foreign military organizations or carrying out missions with local forces in Iraq and Afghanistan, the Green Berets are working to build connections between America and its allies. These connections can often result in valuable intelligence or information that can aid progress toward U.S. goals. In the modern era of military conflicts, the cultural adaptability and language skills that all Green Berets possess are in particularly high demand. Modern Special Forces soldiers work with troops from countries all over the world to improve global security.

After the attacks of September 11, 2001, the Special Forces were called upon to take part in the initial operations of the war in Afghanistan, codenamed Operation Enduring Freedom. With fewer than three hundred Green Berets working alongside local forces, the U.S. Army Special Forces helped topple the Taliban regime after only forty-three days.

Green Berets are involved at the ground level in Afghanistan, speaking with tribal leaders over chai, the local tea, in order to form a bond of trust between the Afghan people and American forces. This sort of work is absolutely vital to the American war effort in Afghanistan, and the Army Special Forces are uniquely prepared for it.

In the war in Iraq, codenamed Operation Iraqi Freedom, the Green Berets have been instrumental in working with local Iraqi soldiers, making partnerships that support U.S. objectives. In the early days of the war, Army Special Forces conducted a number of operations in Western Iraq and helped lead attacks on Saddam Hussein's Baghdad. Special Forces soldiers were later able to prevent troops loyal to the Iraqi dictator Saddam Hussein from reinforcing the capital city of Baghdad by working with U.S.-allied Iraqis.

In addition to their service in the wars in Iraq and Afghanistan, Special Forces soldiers have also partnered with forces in the Philippines and Columbia to fight terrorism and eliminate **insurgencies** in those countries.

The demand for U.S. Special Forces units has grown dramatically in the last decade, and is currently at the highest level in history. In order to address the need for additional Special Forces soldiers, a fourth battalion (of around four hundred soldiers) is being added to each of the five active

UNDERSTAND THE FULL MEANING

insurgencies: Groups of people who are revolting against the government.

Special Forces Groups. Never before has the United States so relied on its Special Forces to conduct operations around the world.

SPECIAL FORCES OPERATIONS

Special Forces operations generally fall into three categories: wartime operations, peacetime operations, and humanitarian missions. These operations may be quite similar. Direct action (a raid on an enemy facility, for example) conducted during wartime may have the intended consequence of disabling an enemy so as to end the war by their defeat. This same mission conducted during a time of peace may have the goal of preventing war from ever taking place by disabling that same enemy capability.

WARTIME OPERATIONS

During times of war, Army Special Forces are most often called upon to employ unconventional warfare tactics, namely guerrilla warfare and the recruitment of local armed forces. The majority of wars are conducted using a combination of both conventional and unconventional warfare. Conventional warfare includes operations on a large scale, using a wide range of vehicles, weapons, and troop units to hit the enemy in a visible way. Unconventional warfare is like a "scalpel" compared to conventional warfare's "hammer." It's designed for delicate but sharp action, and it can have a profound effect on the direction of a war—but is conducted on a smaller scale than conventional war. Guerrilla warfare,

Special Forces troops work closely with local troops in Afghanistan.

a common tactic of unconventional warfare, for instance, often involves quickly attacking enemy forces when they least expect it and then escaping undetected. Other unconventional warfare tactics include raising insurgencies or rebellions within enemy territory and quick strikes on key enemy targets. The U.S. Army Special Forces are among the foremost experts in unconventional warfare in the U.S. military.

One of the key roles of the Green Berets during wartime is to help create insurgencies from within enemy territory. During these missions, Green Berets are often asked to operate on their own, for periods of weeks, months, or even years. Green Berets must make connections with locals in order to gain information and the trust of the people. These soldiers must often work out of uniform. This makes their work extraordinarily dangerous, as the Geneva Convention (which prevents the torture of prisoners of war) only applies to soldiers captured in uniform.

After gaining the trust of local populations, Green Berets must work to identify groups that are displeased with life inside enemy territory, convincing them to rise up against the enemy. Green Berets must train these individuals to combat enemy forces, often organizing and leading them into battle once they are prepared. Building these guerrilla armies can result in increased intelligence gathering from local groups and harm the capabilities of the enemy to wage war.

In addition to creating instability within enemy territory through unconventional warfare, Special Forces soldiers can also assist in targeting enemy facilities, troops, or weapons for conventional attack. In Afghanistan, for instance, Green Berets locate targets that have the most effect when targeted by U.S. missiles. Their ability to remain undetected while assisting conventional forces makes the Green Berets an even greater asset to the current war efforts in Afghanistan and Iraq.

PEACETIME OPERATIONS

While Green Berets operate behind enemy lines during times of war, when the war has ended, they work to build up local institutions and organizations. After a military conflict, the Green Berets who make connections with local groups during wartime are able to assist leaders in reestablishing order and peace. In many ways, Special Forces soldiers are acting as American diplomats abroad when not engaged in combat operations.

TRAINING FOREIGN FORCES

One of the primary ways in which the United States prevents wars from breaking out across the globe is by strengthening its allied nations. By training other nations to defend themselves, whether from foreign or **domestic** threats to security, the Special Forces prevent violent terrorism, drug trafficking, and other potential threats to global stability from spreading. In this capacity, Green Berets work with the governments and military officials from countries around the world as advisors and experts.

UNDERSTAND THE FULL MEANING

domestic: Referring to things within one's own country.

A Special Forces officer coaches a Belizean soldier as he properly zeroes his rifle during a recent marksmanship exercise near Belize City, Belize. The Special Forces members are mentoring their Belizean counterparts in order to help them become a professional special operations unit to combat drug trafficking.

Special Forces train paratroopers from Mali in proper slipping techniques to avoid other parachutists and adjust for wind conditions. This training is part of a special operation designed to build cooperation and unity in Northern and Western Africa. The exercise, which includes participation of key European nations, is conducted by Special Operations Command Africa and is designed to build relationships and develop capacity among security forces throughout the Trans-Saharan region of Africa.

Called Foreign Internal Defense, training foreign military forces in order to assist U.S. allies is a core part of the mission of the U.S. Army Special Forces. As part of their mission to support foreign internal defense, Green Berets are often called upon to train foreign forces, whether police or military organizations.

For instance, Special Forces soldiers train foreign forces in counter-drug operations, in order to stem the flow of illegal drugs on foreign soil, and potentially to the United States. In Belize, U.S. Special Forces soldiers work with the Belizean military to teach them how to prevent illegal drug smuggling across their border. Known mostly as a vacation destination, Belize has become a central location for many drug traffickers. Members from an A-Team from the Seventh Special Forces Group instructs the Belizean forces in a variety of tactics used by the Special Forces soldiers, so that they may better combat drug smuggling. The Green Berets cultural, language, and military knowledge make them the ideal soldiers to take on this kind of work, vital to maintaining global security.

Green Berets are also responsible for many peacetime missions involving the removal and disposal of weapons of mass destruction, though this duty has only been recently given to the Special Forces.

HUMANITARIAN MISSIONS

For the same reasons that Special Forces Soldiers are so uniquely prepared to work with foreign military organizations, create bonds with leaders from other cultures, and

SPARTAN

In the 1970s, the Green Berets even conducted humanitarian missions inside the United States, traveling to poor rural areas in Florida and North Carolina to deliver medical treatment and assist in community development projects. This project was called SPARTAN (Special Proficiency At Rugged Terrain And Nation-Building), and, while short-lived, stands as an example of the unique abilities of Green Berets.

establish connections with soldiers from all over the world, Green Berets are also ideal soldiers to carry out a variety of humanitarian missions. Whether during times of war or peace, humanitarian missions can help strengthen America's hand around the globe. In many cases, winning over local populations during wartime is best done through a combination of **diplomacy** and aid. When not at war, humanitarian efforts ensure that America is seen as a force for good in the world, improving the nation's standing abroad, a key element of maintaining national security.

In the 1980s, Special Forces soldiers guarded the border between Nicaragua and its neighbors Honduras and El Salvador. U.S. officials worried that the Nicaraguan civil war might spread to other countries in the region, igniting vio-

UNDERSTAND THE FULL MEANING

diplomacy: The art and practice of conducting peaceful negotiations between nations.

lence between nations, as well as within them. The Green Berets worked to keep the violent civil war contained within Nicaragua, maintaining peace in the greater area.

In the 1990s, the Green Berets carried out a wide range of operations designed to assist refugees caught in the civil war in Rwanda. Violent conflict put a great many lives at risk at that time, and the Green Berets were called upon to help thousands of people get to refugee camps. Special Forces

U.S. Special Forces in Southern Afghanistan facilitated a medical seminar in which local national medical providers taught both male and female students basic medical knowledge. After completing the three-day seminar, the students linked up with the Afghan medical providers to provide services to their villages.

soldiers also help organize and run these camps, assisting in their administration and operation.

The Green Berets also work to remove unexploded landmines from warzones, one of the most devastating long-term effects war has on a region. After the Vietnam War, for example, one in every 236 people had lost at least a single limb to a landmine left behind after the end of combat. One of the most important humanitarian roles the Green Berets play is in the removal and disposal of unexploded landmines in order to protect civilian populations.

The Green Berets lead Civil Affairs operations for the Army, as well. Civil Affairs (also called CA) work is done by a combination of military and civilian organizations (including nongovernmental organizations (such as the Red Cross) and local political groups. CA operations may include missions such as delivering food aid to starving populations, getting key relief supplies to villages after a war, or ensuring medical supplies are sent to areas in need.

Special Forces Medics in Haiti After the 2010 Earthquake

After the earthquake in Haiti on January 12, 2010, the U.S. armed forces created a **joint task force** to provide humanitarian assistance to the people of Haiti. Special Forces medics were deployed in support of this effort. In makeshift clinics, Special Forces medics, alongside missionaries, workers from nongovernmental organizations, and other Army

UNDERSTAND THE FULL MEANING

joint task force: When units from various branches of the armed services work together to accomplish a specific job.

medics, helped people who needed urgent medical care. In many cases, local hospitals (particularly in the Haitian capital Port-au-Prince, hit hard by the January earthquake) had difficulty caring for the great number of people injured and in need of assistance in the aftermath of the quake.

In June 2010, the task force providing aid to Haiti withdrew its forces, including deployed Special Forces soldiers. The U.S. military, however, remains committed to assisting Haiti in natural disaster relief over the long term. This involves preparing for additional disasters in the future and having a plan for coordinated U.S. relief efforts. Humanitarian work is considered a fulfillment of the Special Forces motto—"To Liberate the Oppressed."

CHAPTER 6

Special Forces Equipment

Though a Green Beret's mind is always his most vital asset, advanced technology and important equipment can provide the support the Army's Special Forces need to complete their missions. Green Berets operate in a wide range of environments, in a variety of conditions, so they must always have—and know how to use—the right gear for any number of circumstances. Each soldier in the Special Forces is trained in how to use a combination of the latest in military-grade technology and more common tools, some even used by civilians.

NIGHT VISION GOGGLES

Night vision goggles allow Special Forces soldiers to see during operations that take place at night or in poorly lit environments. Rather than rely on bringing light with them (flashlights, for instance) the U.S. Army (including the Special Forces) use night vision goggles that **enhance** existing environmental light, as well as **spectrum** not normally visible to the human eye, allowing soldiers to remain unseen by enemy forces, even as they are able to see clearly in the darkest of situations.

One model of night vision goggles used by the U.S. military is the PVS-14 Monocular Night Vision Device. This set of goggles has a single scope as opposed to two—monocular rather than binocular. These goggles carry with them a device called an illuminator that fires a beam of light that the human eye cannot see, allowing a soldier wearing the PVS-14 to see more clearly without being seem by the enemy. A soldier using the PVS-14 views the environment on a screen inside the device. Like many consumer electronic products, the PVS-14 system runs on two AA batteries.

M-4 CARBINE

First used by the U.S. Army in 1997, the M-4 Carbine is both lightweight and highly customizable, making it an ideal weapon for the Special Forces. The M-4 continues the legacy of the Army's standard assault rifle for many years, the

UNDERSTAND THE FULL MEANING

enhance: To increase or improve.

spectrum: The range of colors formed by light based on its wavelengths, only some of which are normally visible to the human eye.

Looking through night-vision goggles, paratroopers search for smugglers and weapon caches in Iraq.

M-16, and before that the M-1 Carbine (used in World War II and the Korean War).

The rifle has a shorter barrel than many other similar weapons, and a collapsible stock, making it excellent for close quarters firing, where soldiers will need a light weapon for quick movement. The M-4 can also be equipped with an infrared sight, allowing increased accuracy. In addition, the M-4 can be outfitted with a M-203 40mm grenade launcher, giving infantry even greater firepower. The M-4 can be customized in many different ways, allowing Special Forces soldiers to use the scopes, lights, or added weaponry that fit any kind of mission. Since the Green Berets may be called to complete missions almost anywhere in the world, weapons that are made to be adaptable can give them the edge while in the field.

LONG RANGE COMMUNICATIONS EQUIPMENT

Special Forces soldiers must be able to communicate with each other at great distances in a variety of ways. These include using text messages, radio transmissions, or satellite computer. Just as instantaneous communication has become vital in the civilian world, the success of the U.S. Army's modern fighting force on the battlefield is based largely on its ability to keep information moving between its units. In the twenty-first century, efficient information flow is vital to any military organization, including the Special Forces.

The M4 is designed to deter, and if necessary, compel adversaries by enabling individuals and small units to engage targets with accurate, lethal, direct fire.

A GPS is one of the modern warrior's tools.

CLIMBING GEAR

Special Forces soldiers may be required to serve in cold-weather, high-altitude environments. In many cases, Green Berets may be called to navigate mountainous terrain in these conditions in order to complete their mission. In these situations, Special Forces soldiers use the same kind of mountain climbing gear used by many civilians who participate in climbing as an extreme sport. This gear includes ice axes, wire stoppers for stopping or slowing descent, and carabiners. Though these items are available to civilians, they are made with safety and functionality in mind.

GLOBAL POSITIONING SYSTEMS (GPS)

Global positioning systems (GPS), used today by civilians across the world, were originally developed for military use. Utilizing a series of satellites, GPS can pinpoint the location of a receiver anywhere on the planet. In the same way that the Internet was first developed by military scientists in order to improve communication within the government and armed services—and then became widely used by civilians—GPS handsets that assist in navigation are used in personal cars, commercial airplanes, and a variety of industrial applications all over the world today.

Green Berets are outfitted with a GPS locator at all times while in the field, so that their position may be monitored. No matter where a soldier is carrying out a mission, GPS ensures that his whereabouts are well known by their superiors should anything go wrong.

SMALL BOATS: KAYAKS, INFLATABLE BOATS

In many missions that involve infiltrating enemy territory by water, Green Berets must use vehicles that are the least likely to be detected by opposing forces. Kayaks, for instance, allow Special Forces soldiers to navigate bodies of water quietly, and move the boat easily. Similarly, lightweight inflatable boats are often used in beach landings to make a quiet insertion into the area in which an operation is to take place. Though often used by civilians and not as technologically advanced as many of the other equipment used by the Special Forces, these methods of transportation offer Green Berets the stealth they so often require in the field.

RE-BREATHERS

While many types of scuba gear provide the diver air from a tank, and then push out exhaled air into the water in the form of bubbles, re-breather systems allow exhaled air to be

Not everything the Green Berets do involves danger and enemy confrontations. These members of the Special Forces Group (Airborne) are providing a Special Forces equipment demonstration at the Atlanta Motor Speedway.

reused, eliminating any need to release bubbles. This allows Special Forces soldiers to travel underwater undetected by any enemies on the surface. Re-breathers work by maintaining a single "breathing loop" that removes carbon dioxide from exhaled air and replaces oxygen that has been consumed. The system also monitors the amount of oxygen the diver is breathing. Scuba gear that emits bubbles operates using what are called open-circuit breathing systems, while re-breathers (which do not expel exhaled air in the form of bubbles) use closed-circuit systems. Green Berets use re-breathers in underwater insertion operations, when moving without detection can be the difference between failure and success, or even life and death.

HIGH-ALTITUDE LOW-OPENING (HALO) HELMET

Green Berets often need to make their entry into enemy territory undetected. In some cases, this requires them to parachute jump from aircraft so high up that soldiers must wear oxygen masks when making their descent. They then open their parachutes very low to the ground, at a height that will allow them to land safely, but also without being seen by enemy radar. This requires these soldiers to wear HALO helmets that provide them with a supply of oxygen during their jump.

Green Berets use special equipment for high-altitude low-opening (HALO) jumps like this, including helmets and specially designed parachutes.

MC-4 PARACHUTE

Specifically designed for the HALO jumps that the Green Berets may be called to perform, the MC-4 parachute is functional even in the extraordinarily severe conditions that Special Forces soldiers may experience during their missions. Special Forces operations can take place in the harshest of environments, and equipment like the MC-4 must be as able to withstand these conditions as the Green Berets themselves.

It takes a lot to make a Green Beret, but extensive training and high-tech equipment are not the most important ingredients. The vital elements of being a Green Beret are excellence and courage, two aspects of the Green Beret's character that are lived out in both wartime and peace.

FIND OUT MORE ON THE INTERNET

Department of Defense www.defense.gov

U.S. Army www.army.mil

U.S Army Airborne School www.benning.army.mil/airborne/airborne

U.S. Army Fort Jackson (Basic Combat Training) www.jackson.army.mil

U.S. Army John F. Kennedy Special Warfare Center and School www.soc.mil/swcs/index.htm

U.S. Army Recruiting www.goarmy.com

U.S. Army Special Forces Command (SFC) (Airborne) www.soc.mil/SF/SF_default.htm

U.S. Army Special Operations Command (SOC) www.soc.mil

The websites listed on this page were active at the time of publication. The publisher is not responsible for websites that have changed their address or discontinued operation since the date of publication. The publisher will review and update the websites upon each reprint.

FURTHER READING

Blehm, Eric. *The Only Thing Worth Dying For: How Eleven Green Berets Forged a New Afghanistan*. New York: Harper Collins, 2010.

Bohrer, David. *America's Special Forces: Seals, Green Berets, Rangers, USAF Special Ops, Marine Force Recon.* St. Paul, Minn.: MBI Publishing Company, 2002.

Department of the Army. *U.S. Army Special Forces Handbook.* New York: Skyhorse Publishing, 2008.

Fowler, Will. *The Special Forces Guide to Escape and Evasion*. New York: St. Martin's Press, 2005.

Neville, Leigh. *Special Operations Forces in Afghanistan: Afghanistan 2001–2007*. Oxford, UK: Osprey Publishing, 2008.

Schumacher, Gerry. *To Be a U.S. Army Green Beret*. St. Paul, Minn.: Zenith Press, 2005.

Stanton, Shelby L. *Green Berets at War: U.S. Army Special Forces in Southeast Asia*, 1956–1975. New York: Ballantine Publishing Group, 1999.

BIBILIOGRAPHY

About.com. "United States Military Weapons of War," usmilitary. about.com/od/armyweapons/l/aainfantry1.htm (7 June 2010).

Fort Campbell. "Welcome," www.campbell.army.mil/units/Pages/ Welcome.aspx (7 June 2010).

GlobalSecurity.org. John F. Kennedy Special Warfare Center, www. globalsecurity.org/military/agency/army/jfksws.htm (7 June 2010).

GlobalSecurity.org. U.S. Army Special Forces Command (Airborne), www.globalsecurity.org/military/agency/army/arsfc.htm (7 June 2010).

GoArmy.com. "Special Forces: Overview," www.goarmy.com/special_forces/index.jsp (7 June 2010).

GoArmy.com. "Special Forces: Training," www.goarmy.com/special_ forces/training.jsp (7 June 2010).

GoArmy.com. "Special Forces: Unconventional Warfare," www. goarmy.com/special_forces/unconventional_warfare.jsp (7 June 2010).

The Global Positioning System. www.gps.gov (9 June 2010).

HowStuffWorks.com. "How Does a Rebreather Work?" science. howstuffworks.com/question632.htm (9 June 2010).

HowStuffWorks.com. "How the Green Berets Work," science.how-stuffworks.com/green-beret.htm (7 June 2010).

HowStuffWorks.com. "How the U.S. Army Works," science.howstuff-works.com/army5.htm (7 June 2010).

Tactical Rebreather Systems. www.tacrs.com/index.htm (9 June 2010).

U.S. Army. "Special Shooters: Shooters and Thinkers," www.army.mil/-news/2009/10/26/29315-special-forces—shooters-and-thinkers/ (7 June 2010).

U.S. Army National Guard. "Military Stays Ready to Respond When Haiti Calls," www.arng.army.mil/News/Pages/MilitaryStaysReadyto-RespondWhenHaitiCalls.aspx (10 June 2010).

U.S. Army Special Forces Command Airborne. www.soc.mil/SF/SF_default.htm (9 June 2010).

U.S. Army Special Forces Command Airborne. "History," www.soc.mil/SF/history.htm (7 June 2010).

U.S. Army Special Forces Command Airborne. "Special Warfare Memorial Statue," www.soc.mil/SF/bruce.htm (7 June 2010).

U.S. Army Special Forces Command Airborne. "Units," www.soc.mil/SF/units.htm (7 June 2010).

U.S. Army Special Operations Command. www.soc.mil (7 June 2010).

U.S. Special Operations Command. www.socom.mil/SOCOMHome/Pages/usasoc.aspx (7 June 2010).

U.S. Army Special Operations Command. "John F. Kennedy Special Warfare Center and School," www.soc.mil/swcs (7 June 2010).

U.S. Army Special Operations Command. "SF Medic Treats Patients at an Improvised Clinic in Cap-Haitien," www.socom.mil/SOCOM-Home/newspub/news/Pages/AnArmySpecialForcesmedictreatspa-tientsatanimprovisedclinicinCap-Haitien,Haiti.aspx (10 June 2010).

U.S. Army Special Operations Command. "Special Forces Train Belizean Forces to Deter Drug Trafficking," www.socom.mil/SOCOM-Home/newspub/news/Pages/SpecialForcestrainBelizeanForcestode-terdrugtrafficking.aspx (10 June 2010).

U.S. Army Special Operations Command. "U.S. Army John F. Kennedy Special Warfare Center and School Fact Sheet," www.soc.mil/swcs/ SWCSfactSheet.pdf (7 June 2010).

U.S. Army Special Operations Command. "USASOC News Service," news.soc.mil (7 June 2010).

U.S. Coast Guard Navigation Center. "GPS General Information," www.navcen.uscg.gov/gps/default.htm (9 June 2010).

INDEX

PICTURE CREDITS

U.S. Army: pp. 8, 13, 30, 32, 39, 41, 44, 47, 48, 51, 57, 59, 62, 66, 69, 70, 73, 76, 79, 81, 82, 85, 87
U.S. Army Center of Military History: p. 11
U.S. Defense Visual Information Center: p. 19
U.S. Department of Defense: pp. 16, 21, 25, 28, 54

To the best knowledge of the publisher, all images not specifically credited are in the public domain. If any image has been inadvertently uncredited, please notify Harding House Publishing Service, 220 Front Street, Vestal, New York 13850, so that credit can be given in future printings.

ABOUT THE AUTHOR

C.F. Earl is a writer living and working in Binghamton, New York. Earl writes mostly on social and historical topics, including health, the military, and finances, among other topics. An avid student of the world around him, and particularly fascinated with almost any current issue, C.F. Earl hopes to continue to write for books, websites, and other publications for as long as he is able.

ABOUT THE CONSULTANT

Colonel John Carney, Jr. is USAF-Retired, President and the CEO of the Special Operations Warrior Foundation.